The Secret Yeltsin Scandal

Discover the truth about the present from events in the past

William Dunkerley

Published by
Omnicom Press
New Britain, CT, USA
Publishers since 1981

www.OmnicomPress.com

ISBN-13: 978-1979533966
ISBN-10: 1979533962
Printed in the United States of America

The Secret Yeltsin Scandal *is part of the "Russia: Straight Talk on Hushed Issues" monograph series. It is dedicated to the concept of a safe, sustaining, and positive relationship between the United States and the Russian Federation.*

A list of other monographs in this series can be found at:

www.OmnicomPress.com/monographs

CONTENTS

Chapter 1
TIPSY BORIS

A stone drunk Boris Yeltsin stood across from the White House in Washington. He was there in his underwear hailing a taxi.

In his stupor, Yeltsin just wanted to go out for a pizza.

You might think this hard-to-believe tale is the secret scandal I'm writing about.

But it's not.

That bizarre incident from the 1990s was recounted earlier in books by Strobe Talbott and Taylor Branch in 2002 and 2009 respectively.

Actually Yeltsin's pizzagate is only an insignificant part of the secret scandal.

Chapter 2
THE REAL SECRET

To uncover the secret Yeltsin scandal we must go back to October 4, 1993.

Moscow was engulfed in a violent, out of control constitutional crisis.

Yeltsin had fired the elected parliament over disagreements. In response Parliament fired Yeltsin. Parliamentarians refused to concede in the standoff.

And when they refused to go, Yeltsin brought in tanks to fire upon them. In all, it was a tragedy that claimed almost 200 lives.

Was That Good or Bad?

Sometime after the tank assault on Parliament,

noted Russian journalist Alexei Pankin discussed it with German colleagues. They tended to support Yeltsin's actions as being fully justified.

Pankin tried to explain that Yeltsin had overstepped his authority when he fired Parliament. The tank attack on Parliament members was an atrocity, he exclaimed.

The Germans reacted to Pankin's explanation with incredulity. It didn't agree with what they had heard. They said, why, if that version were actually true "our German media is engaged in disinformation."

And that's the scandal here. There is widespread distortion afoot. Germany is not alone in doing it. The predominant Western press coverage of the October 4 events embodied serious distortion.

And sadly, the end of the 1993 Moscow constitutional crisis did not signal the end of the false reporting. Distortion became the byword of Western media coverage of Yeltsin. It was all inexplicably lenient and forgiving of the unforgivable.

In stark contrast there is the exceptionally harsh coverage given to Vladimir Putin, his successor.

Chapter 3
WHY THE DIFFERENCE?

As a media professional, I've followed with interest the press coverage of the recent Russian presidents: Boris Yeltsin, Vladimir Putin, Dmitry Medvedev. I have to admit that I've found the nature of the coverage itself to be a bizarre story, one with mystery and intrigue of its own.

Over the years, Yeltsin has been characterized variously as a hero who brought down communism, as the foremost proponent of Russia's transformation to democracy and a market economy, and as a stalwart of Russia's free press. Putin, on the other hand is regarded as a dictatorial tyrant who opposes democracy.

Beyond the popular imagery about Yeltsin, however, there was a less attractive face. Aside from shelling the Parliament, Yeltsin also presided over a looting of state assets, thus creating a circle of newly-minted tycoons that helped to protect the president. Somehow he was able to win reelection in a contest where he held roughly a 5 percent approval rating going into the election season. Ultimately, Yeltsin led the country into a financial collapse near the end of his presidency.

Chapter 4
ADMIRING BORIS

Despite the foregoing, Yeltsin is nevertheless used in many media accounts and in political discourse as a standard of accomplishment against which his successors are being compared.

Notably, Putin is criticized widely in the media for rolling back the democratic gains of the Yeltsin era, for reversing the course Yeltsin had taken away from Soviet-era autocratic rule, and for clamping down on Russia's free press. Typical headlines include "The Rollback of Democracy in Vladimir Putin's Russia" (*Washington Post*) and "How Putin Muzzled Russia's Free Press" (*Wall Street Journal*).

According to my analysis, media accounts seem generally to advance a Yeltsin persona that combines hero, fierce democratic and market

reformer, and relatively harmless drunk.
President Bill Clinton has been quoted observing,
"We can't ever forget that Yeltsin drunk is better
than most of the alternatives sober."

Putin's persona in the press, however, is more
that of a suspicious, power-hungry autocrat who
will stop at nothing, not even murder. On the
PBS *News Hour* with Jim Lehrer, Senator John
McCain once accused Putin's Kremlin of
instituting a "state-run kind of Mussolini style
government."

The Facts

As a case-in-point, I examined the *New York
Times* coverage of Yeltsin's shelling of the
Parliament in 1993. That was one of Yeltsin's
most egregious acts. The *Times* ran a story titled
"SHOWDOWN IN MOSCOW: Tactics; Yeltsin
Attack Strategy: Bursts Followed by Lulls." Here
are some excerpts illustrating how the *Times*
covered the story:

"The assault on the Russian Parliament building
today was a textbook example of the decisive
application of military power...

"And as the daylong assault went on, it was clear
that Mr. Yeltsin's commanders had decided on

gradualism...

"The Russian troops were looking for Bolshoi Devyatinsky lane ... where the defiant lawmakers had maintained their headquarters...

"With the outcome of the battle never in doubt, the clear preference of the military was to scare the anti-Yeltsin demonstrators into surrendering and to limit casualties...

"The only question was the number of lives that would be lost. And that was largely left up to the rebels as they were alternately bombarded with shells and appeals to surrender."

Just note how soft this coverage is. I'm not taking sides on whether Yeltsin's actions were appropriate or not. But, the Yeltsin side is characterized as valiant and measured. The other side is characterized as defiant and to blame for its own fate. The story has a factual basis. The president really did launch a tank assault on the Parliament. However, the circumstances clearly seem to be spun in a way that tempers that stark reality.

Chapter 5
WHAT ABOUT PUTIN?

The flip side of Yeltsin's spun-positive media treatment is the very dark characterizations that are given to Putin. To substantiate that conclusion, I'd like to share with you my investigation into the coverage of Putin's alleged crackdown on Russia's free press, a frequent media theme.

Actually, the press freedom situation is entirely different from how it has been characterized in the Western press.

There never was any free press for Putin to have cracked down on.

Right from the start of the Russian Federation, laws were put into place that assured that. They provided that the media could not achieve the financial strength to be free and independent.

As a result, the press was thrust into the clutches of politicians and business tycoons who propped up the bankrupt media companies in return for the ability to color the news in their own favor.

The media were (and still are for the most part) subjugated, not free. Any reportage claiming there had been a truly free press was either evidence of misunderstanding or falsification.

Another Putin Example

The coverage of the Alexander Litvinenko polonium poisoning offers another textbook case.

In a sense, there are similarities to Yeltsin's battle with Parliament. There is irrefutable evidence that both events actually happened. The attack on Parliament did take place, and Litvinenko was poisoned.

Another similarity is that both stories made the top-stories-of-the-year lists for 1993 and 2006, respectively.

But when you get into the who-did-what-to-whom, the two stories start to become dissimilar in character.

There was lots of evidence that it was Yeltsin who launched the assault on Parliament. With the Litvinenko story, however, there were no journalists who had reliable evidence that Putin was involved. Yet so many stories trumpeted the unsupported allegation that Putin was behind the murder.

In 2007, the organizers of the World Congress of the International Federation of Journalists commissioned me to study the Litvinenko coverage and to report my findings at their meeting. What I found is that most of the popular stories of the time seem to have been based on sheer fabrication. They were all part of a PR blitz cooked up by a disgruntled Russian tycoon.

My investigation ultimately led me to write two books on the Litvinenko case. *The Phony Litvinenko Murder* documents the falsity of media coverage, and *Litvinenko Murder Case Solved* reveals how the British government executed a cover-up of what really happened.

Chapter 6
PUTTING IT IN FOCUS

So, now you have a better picture of the secret Yeltsin scandal.

As you can see, it isn't about the then-president of Russia.

It is really about the media and how they have covered Yeltsin and his successors. It is a scandal of the professional malfeasance of journalists. They have been caught taking shady PR accounts that should have been scrutinized and exploding them into stories of enormous proportion. Just why the media would be united in this ethical transgression defies apparent reason.

It's not been just the Litvinenko story. There's been the incessant stories of how Russia is using energy as a weapon, how there was a rash of journalist murders under Putin, how Russia started a war with Georgia, and on and on. None of these appear to be the whole honest truth, either.

The Outcome?

Whatever happened to Yeltsin's drunken pizza escapade? According to Bill Clinton, "Yeltsin got his pizza."

As to the real Yeltsin scandal, the shoddy, phony journalism regarding Russia?

That one is still unfolding. Too many journalists are still taking a slipshod approach to reporting. It's come to be called fake news.

Going forward, as you read reportage about Russia, keep in mind "The Secret Yeltsin Scandal."

Look for factual substantiation of those future reports, positive or negative!

Appendix I
THE AUTHOR

William Dunkerley is a media business analyst and Senior Fellow at American University in Moscow. He has worked on behalf of US interests in promoting press freedom in Eastern Europe and the former Soviet Union. He was commissioned by the International Federation of Journalists to analyze problems in certain Western press coverage of Russian issues. Mr. Dunkerley has been instrumental in shaping laws governing the media in Eastern Europe and Russia and has offered testimony to the United States Congress on media concerns. He has personally done intensive work in seven post communist countries, including interventions in seventeen different cities across all Russia. He is principal of William Dunkerley Publishing Consultants, and publisher of two industry monthlies, *Editors Only* and the *STRAT* newsletter.

Appendix II
THIS SERIES

"Russia: Straight Talk on Hushed Issues" is a monograph series that looks behind the popular headlines and presents iconoclastic analyses. The books explain aspects of mainstream news that are either being distorted, glossed over, or hushed up.

The etiology of these media distortions is complex. Historically there was little harshness in the coverage of Yeltsin's misdeeds, perhaps a result of Western giddiness over the collapse of the Soviet Union.

When Putin entered the scene in 1999 the kid gloves came off. He was demonized. Russian tycoons who had been involved in skullduggery under Yeltsin found the new leader problematic.

Boris Berezovsky, one of the tycoons, carried

media attacks to new heights after fleeing to London in 2001 to evade corruption charges. He packaged and distributed highly engaging news stories with associated graphics and interview opportunities to media outlets worldwide. Probably because of that convenience, they were readily accepted by the media unquestioningly despite their lack of factual bases.

Inexplicably, after Berezovsky's 2014 death, the stream of demonizing stories continued. Had Berezovsky's campaign just made an indelible impression that still taints the views of media and political leaders in the US and elsewhere? Or is there a new kingpin yet to be identified?

Regardless, many people have indeed formed beliefs based on the prevalence of distorted news and are committed to them. It would be unrealistic to think many of these folks will accept any contravening facts and analyses.

So the intention of this series is to give open-minded audiences in the US and other Western countries insights into misleading and fabricated reportage. That should allow them to arrive at more realistic and fact-based understandings, thus facilitating their serving more responsibly as members of our society. The intention is not to exonerate anyone who has been accused, but to point out that the accusers are liars and fabricators. (Note: Monographs in this series appear in no particular order.)

H.G. Wells once said: "Civilization is in a race between education and catastrophe."

But what is now unfolding in the theater of US-Russia relations is a race between catastrophe and utter disaster.

One entrant is the United States, and the other is Russia. Which country is on which side actually makes no difference. In this race, there are allegations, then sanctions, and then retributions for the previous actions. It is a self perpetuating loop.

This is a race in which the winner will personify either political buffoonery or plain stupidity. And which of the two is the victor will also make no difference. The main point for the rest of us is that this race will cause us all to lose.

As part of the "Russia: Straight Talk on Hushed Issues" monograph series, this book is dedicated to ending that foolish race, and to the concept of a safe, sustaining, and positive relationship between the United States and the Russian Federation.

Appendix III
ACKNOWLEDGMENT

In the face of much media misinformation about Russia, I wish to acknowledge the effort and perseverance of all who have spoken and written the honest truth. They have shown great courage in bucking the unfortunate mainstream trend toward fabrication. Their work serves as an essential predicate to this book. --W.D.

www.ingramcontent.com/pod-product-compliance
Lightning Source LLC
Chambersburg PA
CBHW061929270726
48660CB00003BA/1111